Ranchero Ford/
Dying in Red Dirt Country

Ranchero Ford/ Dying in Red Dirt Country

W.K. Stratton

ISBN: 978-1-942956-07-5
Library of Congress Control Number: 2015945362

Lamar University Press
Beaumont, Texas

For LCP

&

once again,

for HAE

Books from Lamar University Press

Jean Andrews, *High Tides, Low Tides: the Story of Leroy Colombo*
Charles Behlen, *Failing Heaven*
Alan Berecka, *With Our Baggage*
David Bowles, *Flower, Song, Dance: Aztec and Mayan Poetry*
Jerry Bradley, *Crownfeathers and Effigies*
Terry Dalrymple, *Love Stories, Sort Of*
Chip Dameron, *Waiting for an Etcher*
Robert Murray Davis, *Levels of Incompetence: An Academic Life*
William Virgil Davis, *The Bones Poems*
Jeffrey Delotto, *Voices Writ in Sand*
Gerald Duff, *Memphis Mojo*
Ted L. Estess, *Fishing Spirit Lake*
Mimi Ferebee, *Wildfires and Atmospheric Memories*
Ken Hada, *Margaritas and Redfish*
Michelle Hartman, *Disenchanted and Disgruntled*
Michelle Hartman, *Irony and Irreverence*
Katherine Hoerth, *Goddess Wears Cowboy Boots*
Lynn Hoggard, *Motherland, Stories and Poems from Louisiana*
Dominique Inge, *A Garden on the Brazos*
Gretchen Johnson, *The Joy of Deception*
Gretchen Johnson, *A Trip Through Downer, Minnesota*
Laozi, *The daodejing*, tr. David Breeden, Steven Schroeder, Wally Swist
Christopher Linforth, *When You Find Us We Will Be Gone*
Tom Mack and Andrew Geyer, editors, *A Shared Voice*
Jim McJunkin, *Deep Sleep*
Dave Oliphant, *The Pilgrimage, Selected Poems: 1962-2012*
Janet McCann, *The Crone at the Casino*
Erin Murphy, *Ancilla*
Kornelijus Platelis, *Solitary Architectures*
Harold Raley, *Louisiana Rogue*
Carol Coffee Reposa, *Underground Musicians*
Jim Sanderson, *Trashy Behavior*
Jim Sanderson, *Sanderson's Fiction Writing Manual*
Jan Seale, *Appearances*
Jan Seale, *The Parkinson Poems*
Carol Smallwood, *Water, Earth, Air, Fire, and Picket Fences*
Glen Sorestad, *Hazards of Eden, Poems from the Southwest*
Melvin Sterne, *The Number You Have Reached*
John Wegner, *Love is Not a Dirty Word and Other Stories*
Robert Wexelblatt, *The Artist Wears Rough Clothing*
Jonas Zdanys, *Pushing the Envelope*

For more information about these and other books, go to
www.LamarUniversityPress.Org

Acknowledgments

"Dying In Red Dirt Country" appeared in its entirety in *Iron Horse Literary Review*. I'm indebted to Leslie Jill Patterson, the editor of *Iron Horse*, for publishing such a long (very long) poem.

I am grateful to the editors of *Rusty Truck, Maintenant,* and *Agave* for publishing other poems included in this book.

CONTENTS

Part II: Dying in Red Dirt Country

Foreword
by Chuck Kinder

Ranchero Ford/Dying in Red Dirt Country is a Sam Peckinpah western movie of a book, part *Junior Bonner* (1972), part *Ballad of Cable Hogue* (1970), a mélange of memoir and powerful poetry, beautifully lyrical, without ever being pretty.

Imagine if you would, gentle reader, old Bloody Sam Peckinpah holed up for his final days in the Murray Hotel in Livingston, Montana, crazy on cocaine, whiskey and regret as he writes not the final script of his thunderbolt life, but a book of poetry, pausing occasionally only to shoot at his own reflection in mirrors or flies on the walls

This is that book of poems, poems about being brave in the face of wreckage, waste and lost hope, poems that blaze with August afternoon heat, under cloudless skies yellow with relentless sun, feverish with daydreams of lost visions. Poems peopled with loners and losers, lost, forsaken souls who long to be honorable and idealistic, but are forced instead to compromise in order to survive in a world of nihilism, brutality, drought, and failed crops.

Poems written in the late, great Richard Hugo language of lost landscapes. Poems that read like tombstones in gunfighter boothills, graveyards thick with Johnson grass and copperheads.

No country for lawmen or timid poets.

Now all this amazingly original, groundbreaking book of poetry needs to be perfect is the perfect soundtrack. But Bloody Sam had already preciously employed Bob Dylan, the most obvious first choice, to compose the soundtrack for *Pat Garrett & Billy the Kid* (1973).

So, imagine once again, please, gentle reader, a kitchen table late at night, surrounded by a posse of bearded poets drinking shots of Old Forester straight from a bottle they pass between them. These bearded gentlemen are also passing a doobie as thick as a gunfighter's wrist.

Also these bearded bards are picking old, battered guitars as one of them, who looks just like Willie Nelson, reads out loud from Bloody Sam's only book of poems. The other bearded gentlemen you begin to recognize as Waylon Jennings, Merle Haggard, Johnny Cash, Bob Wills, and there's even Tom Waits and Tom Petty. Neil Young by God! Plus there is a clearly dead man sitting at that kitchen table they all simply call Hank.

Like the amazing poems that inspired it that soundtrack is hauntingly lovely and elegiac without ever being sentimental or maudlin.

Every note true, sad, tough and brave.

Quite simply I goddamn love this wonderful book. It is like none other I have ever read.

Chuck Kinder's most recent books are *All That Yellow* and *Imagination Motel*. He is also author of the contemporary classic novel *Honeymooners: A Cautionary Tale*, which was drawn from his longtime friendship with Raymond Carver. His other books include *Snakehunter* and *Last Mountain Dancer*.

Introduction

So words have two meanings, sometimes, but it becomes increasingly clear, as the years shudder onward, that they have no meaning at all for too many people. I find that I exist on several planes of time simultaneously—say, today, 1973, and 1913. I'd like to tell you it's the result of Owsley acid or peyote, but I'm afraid it's just my pathology. Right now I'm watching *Pat Garrett & Billy The Kid* for the first time in the dust at the long-deceased Melba; and I'm staring at Pancho Villa as he strolls toward me, *pistola* drawn, pith helmet punched back; and I'm listening to some high-tech narcissist slaughter the definition of the word curator. It's now been 31 years since I last saw the HAE to whom this book is co-dedicated, 31 years since he took his last walk. Yet I talked to him this morning in a beer joint, affectionately remembered as the TIT (Travel In Tavern). Later I drove around Austin, Texas, as it was in 1975 during my first visit here, even as the pestilence twins of wilt and bulldozer destroy much of what I have loved about this place.

I don't want to discuss stability.

Death and decay shaped many of these pages. I'm deep in a funeral parlor season; I can't pretend it will end soon. That's the phase of this particular plane and this particular pain, sealed urns and open caskets. Or maybe it is the phase of every plane I've ever occupied. When I was a green newspaper reporter, I saw a man who'd been murdered with a hog butchering knife. He sat on a mound of trash in his living room, eyes frozen on me, a half-burned cigarette between his fingers. Chickens pecked around his feet. I revisit him mornings as I stand before the shaving mirror. I did so today.

Four years ago, a book of mine appeared called *Dreaming Sam Peckinpah*. This book, *Ranchero Ford/Dying in Red Dirt Country*, can stand alone, but it should be considered volume two of a larger work of which *Dreaming Sam Peckinpah* is volume one.

I'm grateful to many people for all they have done for me over the years. I'll mention a few names: Kenny Walter first saw a writer in me, saw

13

that my poems might have value, and I'm appreciative for that and for decades of guidance and friendship. Bill Lehmann was the first person to pay me to write; I'll always be beholden. Roxie Powell and Charles Plymell are steadfast in their support, as is A.D. Winans. Many editors have been generous in publishing my work, but I want to thank Peter and Kat at Three Rooms in particular. Liza and Harry—well, in different ways, they saved me.

WKS

Part I: Ranchero Ford

Ranchero Ford

i.

Roll you down to house-trailer days—
And rutted alley grease
And abandoned cutting torches
And rusted skies.

He contains no memory of that now.

His fingers are purple radishes.
His nails are steer horns.
His knuckles are coal chunks
That neglected diamonds.

His eyes expired into gouges
Too horrible for knifework.
He never learned to cry.
Except once. For a dog.

He cannot be dying.
He is dying.

ii.

Put you down to leather on spike
And your thighs bruise striped
For things you never did, wrong or right,
In days when dust never ceased.

That damn shop, belt on wall,
Endless air-compressor explosion,
Creepers on the floor,
Transmission fluid firing my nose.

For him model came first, then make,
The old mechanic's way:
Bel Air Chevy, Skylark Buick, 88 Olds,
DeVille Cadillac, Ranchero Ford. . .

Ranchero Ford.

iii.

A rust-bin:
My bedroom
Hangs above it.

Dropped Ranchero
In wrecker lot.
Bed of peeled parts—
Carburetors, valves,
Tappet covers,
Brake shoes,
Fan belt serpents,
Glitter in thunderstorms:

The only diamonds
In this vicinity.

Twice a year
He hauls the gathering
To the junkyard
Next to the roundhouse.

I breathe
Orange metal
As I sleep.

iv.

Your sister rides Arizona
And Alaska and Wyoming.
You never saw her black eyes.

You never battled her.
You never confessed her.
You never knew her to love her.

You own no letters.
You bathe in air.
Take you down
And no one opens doors.

Just a two and a half ton
          wrecker
In dry night, winch squeals,
Cable swirls, trooper cars,
Flashlights and dance
Of red and blue domes
Outside the lot gate.

Only weight to abide.

v.

One night you jump
The Ranchero alive.
One night you brave
Razor seat springs
And wheel through gates
On flat tires.

One night this repository
Only for scrap
Propels you to highway
Escapes
No one believes its sound.
You flee it abandoned
At the S.H. 33 junction.

He is pissed.

vi.

Ranchero Ford
And the sum of his
Combustion.

You've seen him ablaze
Literally
Twice in the shop war zone.

Another time
A gas tank explodes,
His head a flame nest.

You missed that one
But you witnessed
His radiator scalding,

Forehead pounded by car hoods,
Hands seared on engine heads,
Feet crunched by rolling wheels,

Ribs shattered by falling
          transmissions—
Carnage consistently
Yet he failed his exit—

vii.

Until this night,
All threats hammered,
Save the decades.
Ranchero Ford—

It withstands behind chainlink,
Black locust piercing its bed,
Camouflaged by Johnson grass,
Vandal spiderwebbed windshield.

He falls away
Far from the way.
You inhale.
But scrap cannot reckon.

viii.

Take you down to a dream
Of your missing sister
Appaloosa mounted
In Wyoming breeze and frost.

Take you down to highway
Miles totaled and retotaled—
New Mexico/Utah/Arizona/
Colorado/Montana/Idaho/
Utah/Oregon/Washington/
Rolled and misspent:
Texas/California/
Red dirt solder in the treads:
Ceaseless.
Unbreakable.

Take you down, take you down:
Ranchero Ford unmovable.

He wears your tie in the box.

ix.

Red dirt visage
In the independence month.
Faces wind-sanded to years
          ahead of years.
A concrete lined gap
And the howl of summer bugs.

Lower you down
Lower us down
Lower him down.

Clay envelopes our least
Below this hill
Amid gunfight monuments.

x.

And so you fire his S&W .38
Into the Ranchero Ford
that midnight.

No ricochet, no sparks,
Just a summer dead groan—
More weight to contain.

And so it shall be:
Ranchero Ford,
Wreckage everlasting.

Near Turkey Creek

Here is the Ringer house on the hill,
Hammered sandstone and shingles:
Inside an old woman dissolves into
        a question mark
While her daughter sips vinegar.

Down by Turkey Creek is where
The son lives, wife and seven children,
And a sagging T of a house, three rooms,
Sharecropper leaks and field rats.

But it is his. He preaches it to himself.

For thirteen years the old woman rots
While still breathing, never escaping
Her plastered room—not a crack—
Leaving her daughter to tote piss and plop

To the outhouse in a gallon syrup can
Four times a day. The sun burns nothing.
She squints when she sees how her brother
Oils his curls and dances behind the team.

She squints and it grinds: Her life reduced
To an old woman's snore and fleeting gas.
But one morning mother's skin is butter cool,
Her eyes fixed on the perfect plaster.

The bed is spent. But the daughter owns papers.

She also owns a Ford, which she cranks to town.
First the bank, then the lawyer, then the undertaker.
The undertaker makes the trip with two helpers.
They plod by mule, the Ford impatient behind.

The helpers rein the mules to the rock house

27

And open the doors to the hearse for the box.
The lifeless question mark cannot lie straight
So they break her back and legs with a hand sledge
        to get her into the casket.

The brother watches from coffee bean shade,
Knowing while not knowing, certain but—
He remembers he owns no papers:
Wife and seven children, but no papers.

Just one day later, Roselawn opens for
        the dead woman.
Brother and sister stare at each other
        over the hole.

The sky is yellow.

The lawyer arrives at the three-room house
The next day and toes at the chickens.
Here is a paper, here is a Bugle Boy
        tobacco can
With rolls of fifty dollar bills.

You have a week to vacate, Fred.
The brother gazes up the hill at the rock house.
Is she watching? Answers mean nothing.
He grabs a hatchet from near the kindling mound.

The lawyer leaps back but the brother turns away.
He spreads his hand on the chopping mound
And takes off two fingers with a swipe.
The lawyer trembles and chokes his snuff wad.

The brother shoots crimson across his tie.

Damn fool thing to do, Fred, damn fool!
Reckon so, he says. But she's done.
He turns back to the rock house in long shadow.

The windows are empty. Dead fingers gray
       on the chopping stump.

Two weeks later they arrive in Arkansas
On a Greyhound bus, wife melted,
Children sick from the jostle,
His swollen hand slung in his overalls bib.

This is my blood.

Absolution

Holes swallow caverns below these leaves.
Drought-dying live oaks await bulldozer blades.
This is Austin, Texas, as it never should be.
Unsanctified heat pierces your worn soles.
How did they choose this? How can they breathe?
Everything is forgotten here, worse than L.A.
You wonder about it all—stacks of condos everywhere.
They come and continue, each a new monument
        to empty cube trays and bad, bad love.

You are guilty—careless with her gifts.
How can you fit yourself into that hollowness?

You brain burns this question when he appears:
The G-string man on his Schwinn bicycle.
Yes, you've seen him before from afar.
But now he blocks your sidewalk.
He wears a knit codpiece, gladiator sandals,
        a Bat Masterson hat.
His legs are unpainted pencils.
Gray Persian tail fur covers his chest.

Before you speak, he lifts both fists.
And then he spreads his fingers.
Released starlings, ten Duncans fly before you.
He has looped one to each digit.
They spit and whirl around your face.
An eternity, it seems—before they stop.

Then the creak of pedals on an August afternoon.
A Schwinn seat stabs his ass.
The ten yoyos caress the worn handlebars.
He slides up Shoal Creek Boulevard.

She is endless blue water deep in limestone.
You flee all this to tumble her embrace.

Influenza at Christmas

Vaccines collapse and abandoned
Childhood pain inches its return.
Too many rooms, too many faces
Intrude on congestion dimmed
Logic. You shiver and hide it.
O joyous night, O bedecked halls,
And gray city traffic water,
Then a bed that declines warmth.
Come on, smile, you'll feel better—
But you want to smack all voices.
You want to free the beating inside.
You want to give up a clean Christmas.

A stroke sent him to a coma far away.
Seven lightless years until its release.

Wind in Oklahoma

We called him Chief, a Pawnee in khakis.
He salted his Busch Bavarian.
He taught me to use a crappie sinker.
He gave me a tackle box and short rod.
He opened Martin Lake's muddy water.
I saw fish hidden below sandstone waves.

We called him Chief.
No one spoke his name.

Tonight I learn of oilfield slaughter
And a three-year-old killed
By a highway patrol bullet.
Tonight you celebrate bulldozer holidays
Though wheat is drought-killed
And cattle prices are just as dead.

You wonder how you lost me.
I say Chief died nameless somewhere.
You miss my point.

I listen to Billy Joe Shaver
And raise a beer to Chief.
He understood I craved tracks and highways,
Anything that fell from your wind.

Leaving John Graves

I drove over a fucking shovel
Leaving John Graves' funeral—
Right in the middle of the highway.
The sky bled the same colors
As Interstate 35. I condemned
The road crew bastard
Who, scurrying to beat the rain,
Dropped his tool in the lanes.

You motherfucker—
$500 in repairs down the line.
Choke on your beer at Papa Joe's.

Now I fight overpass torrents
Waiting for someone to tell me
Everything I have done wrong while
Recalling a San Angelo rancher
Who said to me, All it takes to kill
Drought is one good thunderstorm.
Could this be it? I doubt it.
My famine will linger forever.

I close the light and conjure
Graves in the Brazos canoe.
His one eye caught the red-wing
Blackbird's dip across the river.
He spat tobacco but fumbled
The camera tucked next to the dog.
No matter: The photo evaporated
Before it could develop.

Here is the real album:

Texas, our Texas is doublewide
Mobile home halves in highway tow.
It is wind turbines, it is relay spears,

It is wadded tires, it is closeout malls,
It is discount graveyards, it is screw fast motels,
It is airport thieves, it is pickpocket clinics,
It is credit card cathedrals, it is high
          occupancy lanes,
It is programmed country music,
It is Western boots assembled in China,
It is $400 denture outlets,
It is cablevision rodeos,
It is salsa mild in cellophane,
It is toll roads guided by Spain,
It is corrupt well-scrubbed rest stops,
It is abandoned Indiana license plates,
It is authentic New Jersey pizza signs—
Texas, our Texas.

A storm shift and a housing development
Appears like broadcast grain sorghum
Along a forgotten distant creek.

I stir, start my engine, ignore warning
          lights—
That fucking shovel—
And drive away, aching for exit.

Cocaína

She stacks one day ahead of the last.
Each breath shoves the next.
She scours every eight hours.
Her favorite color is soaked concrete.
Tattoos repulse her.
Her skin is a fresco, Huaxtek Studios.
She misses freckles.
She misses her sister.
Her eyes fail word lines.
She wishes she'd been named Gabriela.
She thanks the soil she's never been struck.
She forsook her photographs.
She misplaced her in-call breeze.

Night brings dissolution ink.
Sweat and shiver fuse.
Another fence slices the sky.
She wants for time.

Antlers Inn: 1979

Someone plays Crystal Gayle through
This whiskey lobby haze. We are all
Ready for times to get better.

I cannot sing.

Two hours earlier she told me
About beer joint death, no bullets
In the gunshot asphalt corpse.

Her eyes froze gray.

I saw the kid spread against
Inch-deep black water,
Deputies stubborn against failure:

Little Dixie.

Stories never grow here.
Tomorrow we drive through
      Weyerhauser trees
Toward Choc beer and lamb fries.

Will she survive?

Answers burn my eyelids.
I will not speak them.
I will not reveal my tracks—

Condemned to know,
Condemned to breathe.

Leaving Comanche Territory

The pre-fab full Gospel tabernacle
Steeple tilts rusted in afternoon sun.
I am as alone as I have ever been.
Trailer houses nestle truck-sized hay bales
And women hide window-shade tears as train
Moans promise nothing but grass fire warnings.
Welcome To Outlaw Country
Reads the sign outside the high school.
The Dairy Queen has been converted
Into a mayor's office and city hall.
Living is flat here. Comanches celebrated
This place. They thrived in this dust
With buffalo company after slave raids
Along the New Mexico borderland.
But I cannot seize it.
I can only daydream their lost visions
While the highway draws me toward
The river. I push my pedal over the bridge
To the wet promise she holds in other country.

On the Western Slope, 1979

We wake outside Telluride in summer denial.
A couple rolls naked on the grass next to us.
We slept in clothes at her insistence.
We are from Oklahoma.
People come here this month for bluegrass.
But I am here for trout and weed. She is lost.
She is the wadded drawing of herself tossed
        into last night's piñon flames.

The naked woman's breasts flush the sun.
She has never walked a step in Oklahoma.
I am chided for watching her breaths.
I am chided, I am chided, I am chided.
Across this campground someone plays
        breakfast music:
A new song by the Cars: "The Dangerous Type."
She is indeed a lot like you.

We are too high.
We are too early.

My only hope is just the right pool,
        waist deep water, trout vision.
I'll tie on a nymph at first, which won't work.
I'll try popper promise.
I'll mediate each cast.
But I'll be wondering how it is to sleep naked
        beneath Telluride's summer frozen stars.

She produces new paper.
She begins sketching herself anew.
I fling my waders over my shoulders
And begin the long hike up Skunk Creek.

Leon Russell in 1965

Here we know brass and wood.
Six dozen of us gathered
Through cigarette fog and
Union complaints—

But the piano bench looms empty.

All tuning concluded,
All scores adjusted,
We lean five minutes
Beyond the start of time.

Then he emerges.

Wolfman hair in those days
And Satan's beard,
Legs like sprung pipe cleaners:
Oklahoma childhood polio, they say.

(No one hurried him back then.
No one heard him speak a word.
No one knew the fount of those
        Baptist chords.)

He limps across the room.
We eye each step slide.
He twists onto the bench.
He works his thumbs like puppets.

Leon, drills the voice
Shielded by four-inch glass,
*Leon, let's be on time
For future sessions.*

He fingers the knobs
As if they connect every

Lost California picture card
To dead Tulsa sleet storms.

The fallboard descends
With octave master digits
And he is on his virus hobble
           back out—
Past us, the six dozen, watching,

Never saying anything
As he hitches his way
Into the cymbal crash
Of L.A. afternoon traffic

Not a single note proffered.

Pat Garrett & Billy the Kid at The Melba

Tonight you compress into mildewed cushions.
Mesas and arroyos etched postcards from four years ago.
You wore them to crinkled smears beneath your pillow.
But here they bleed alive again—
        Pat Garrett & Billy the Kid release on the screen.
Melba Theater, Harrison Avenue, Guthrie, Oklahoma:
So many movies, so many escapes, RC Cola
        in waxed paper cups, all those nights—
But you've never obtained anything like this.

And it's not just you.

Some guy ignites a Marlboro and smokes.
No one has ever done that before in the Melba.
He doesn't care; he's long gone in the celluloid.
The theater manager doesn't care either.
This is *Pat Garrett & Billy the Kid*.
The Western is buried unembalmed.
We cannot be the same.

And then you drift into the after-credits night.
Kristofferson's bullet hole is your third tit.
Yet you pray you could be James Coburn,
        nothing but angles and silver and water eyes.
But there's no chance of that, not here.

Lonnie and Gene's is the barbershop at the corner.
The four-lane bowling alley rattles across the street.
Buck Owens echoes from Edna's Lounge.
You smell the sweat of sandstone buildings.
Sheet lightning burns a blackened horizon.

And now a pickup shudders past, silent, except
        for the cricket crackle beneath its tires.
The coal bugs coat the roads this time of year.
The story is ancient as this town.

You slump into your Ford.
You'll add to the slaughter.

Later you lie awake in a twin bed, wagon wheel
       footboard, Indian bedspread.
No sleep can come: crickets scream from every corner.
In the dim gray you make out Cream and Led Zeppelin
       on your walls.
You own nothing but a hollow gut.
You rise and pare the posters in the dark.
You can collect the pieces at dawn.
But for now, you pry open the bedside window.
You climb out into the old man's junkyard—
Seventeen years old in white underwear—
Aglow beneath a graduation moon,
Thigh-deep in Johnson grass and copperheads,
Rolling toward a thunderstorm-strong wind
Beyond the rusted Ramblers and Skylarks,
You pierce the six-feet of faulty chain-link
       to Oklahoma Avenue:

I ran four miles that night before the rains came.
Dead crickets blistered my bare feet.
But I tripped home for the first time. . .

Beer House Memory

Once again a Beer House memory
And the sorrow of Christmas Eve.
And then pickup drive and swoop
To etched-gray gathering family.
A manufactured sister-in-law
Presents the unwrapped gift:
Willie Nelson *Sings Kristofferson.*
For a final time you see her smile.

Ponder these later years—your face
Is a bad plaster resemblance
And her brain breeds cancer. Some weeks
The daughters extend her by wheelchair.
You can't visit it. May we all die free.

Kristofferson folds in on himself nowadays
But Willie sings Indian casinos upward:
Fortitude of a sort.
          And still that Beer House memory—
You comb clay for deliverance dawn.

Coda: Tuco and Blondie

Consider this: Tuco is holding gold—
Undreamable riches—a noose, a cross.
True, he is bound and horseless
And encircled by graveyard markers.
True, he has no water.
But we have seen him exploded.
We have seen him dive through glass
            clutching meat and wine.
We have seen him tortured.
We have seen him escape and rise.
It is within our conception, then:
He will transport *el oro* to Mexico.
He will absorb markets.
He will place money with wisdom.
He will boast of wives in nine parishes.
His hacienda will spread like
            quicksilver.
Peons will not preclude him.

Here is his portrait in oil now:
Black sombrero, black jacket,
Conches colored like mountain lakes.
Yet his eyes fall short of contentment.

We understand:
Blondie abides.

Blondie dreams those nights
When he was known as no one
And bedded women the way some men
Devour saltines. His teeth are missing.
Unshavable whiskers sprout on his wattle.
He shivers a norther in an Oak Cliff
            boarding house
And whispers about money shaken free.
He loathed automobiles, sank funds

44

Into Texas' largest harness company.
He pulls a moth riddled sweater tight.
He recalls a man snakebit while haying.
That's acceptable, a venom blackness,
But not this dissolution. Where is that currency?
Tuco's heart beats within his own chest.
Someone said Tuco was rich south of the river.

Ice will form these windows tonight.

He nods, then awakes, fingers too shaky
            for the trigger.
A trashcan topples in wind wail.
He hears glass crack in the alley,
Boot steps on the black moon stairway.

Riding in Karen Valentine's Mustang

Shadows short, echoes recoiled,
And it's only Gentleman Jim and I
Alive in Karen Valentine's Mustang.
A day rolls from Dirty Martin's Place
And we murmur along
Beyond Jayne Mansfield's boarding house
Over neglected leaves—
And beer would be fine
But Gentleman Jim is dry,
Pugilist still training
Five decades after the ring.
I propose the size of Mansfield's breasts,
Gawked at in my stepbrother's *Playboys*,
Before he left for Vietnam.
Then we make it past Farah Fawcett's
   sorority house—

And afternoon is golden as a full moon.
Karen Valentine's Mustang is blue
As a high school girl's dream eyes.
She drove it during her *Room 222* exaltation.

   She and her husband and Jim worked
   Together at an electronics plant,
   Snapping components while awaiting
   Film and television invitation.
   Then she created times big
   And Gentleman Jim wound up
   Paying her $500, then theft and recovery
   And maybe a paint job, and all is good
   And profound this day. . .

Our target is Lake Austin Inn—
Old suspension of Gentleman Jim
And Timmy Overton's thugs
And Bergstrom flyboys

And UT girls out to scramble
1960s boredom. . .

Of course Lake Austin Inn
Crumbled into bullion
Decades ago but maybe
Its light lingers.
(They say raccoons waltzed the floors.)
Besides it's good to hum along in
Karen Valentine's hardtop,
Though mansion wreckage awaits.
And somewhere, we know,
Darrell K Royal counts exhalation.
   I think about the last time I saw him:
    Smiling at El Patio, glad to be lost. . .
And who wouldn't be, in this diamond
Rubble, where everything has dropped
To nothing, except Karen Valentine's
Dust blue Mustang?

Damn, it is a badge to be with
Gentleman Jim, splicing Tarrytown,
Ford brakes dragging, no matter,
As we aim for the low water crossing:
Then climbing toward Wildcat Hollow—
In the day, cedar choppers fought dogs
In these trees, but now "four bedrooms/
   four baths" is squalor.
The brakes drag more and we creep,
Enraged SUVs on the missing tailgate,
Fingers flashing out windows—
   California assholes, Jim declares,
And maybe he's right:
But Karen Valentine's Mustang blasts
   vindication, somehow—

And the afternoon remains lunar gilt
And Gentleman Jim is my great friend
And we can live.
We cease at gated enclaves.
Jim points out where Lake Austin Inn
Collapsed when Timmy's hoods knifed
The sun out off a fall morning.
Now its sinew lifts lawn manicures.
Across the lake khakied men
In tassel shoes sip lattes
Where once Mean Gene of the Green Machine
Was shot by a chubby lawyer's kid—
Blood commas in guacamole waves
But Mean Gene was too tough to die.
The docks never made it, though,
And the latte men disdain their view,
Samsung prayers to shelved skeletons,
Karen Valentine's Mustang on a rise.
Gentleman Jim and I—we defy all exits.

The Dead

You slip away to Oklahoma City
through frost and shiver. Cusp of seventeen
and alone, 1964 Ford Galaxy
that coughs and rolls—all the windows collapse
if you slam the door, souvenir
of the mescaline summer. Hair flooding
your collars these nights, new Tony
Lamas with leather soles like roller skates,
pipe-leg Levi's and you're a sight,
wireframe glasses and plaid C.P.O.
that might as well be weed smoke. Yes,
a sight, the living far from clean. First
stop, Mother's Rock Shop, full
of patchouli women, as you'd hoped, but not
a one casting an eye your direction.
Bongs and papers and underground ink—
is that thunder?—but you're upstairs
soon enough. You buy this month's
grail, Grateful Dead Europe '72,
and then back to the Galaxy to twist your way
downtown. Civic Center Music Hall,
all hair and tie-dye and buckskin:
You lock Europe '72 in the trunk,
not that freaks steal, and head inside
for endless tuning: Welcome to the Cowboy Kid.

Cops expel beach balls and Frisbees,
harsh, but it's Oklahoma City.
Forever is a walk to Norman and back.
Finally it is done and lights contract into
serpents along the aisles. It is the Dead,
Pig sick and locked away, but the Dead.
The Dead. Patchouli women grow in the aisles,
liberated tits a-sway beneath
peasant blouses, hair blossoms swirling,
bare feet flying over concert

49

venue carpet. And the Cowboy Kid
falls into it, speared through the heart
by Garcia's guitar, climbing each inch
of dark air to the ceiling. Not even the OKC
cops will mess with patchouli women and their
endless smiles. And your own flight?
You've winged it without so much as a twitch.
Three and a half hours later you hang
aloft still, the Cowboy Kid a sky
banner, no more garage creepers, no grease
guns, no ratchets, no air compressors. At last.

Junior High Keys

Criminal introduction: All you do
Is steal junior high keys. Borrowed Yamaha
Roar to the Ben Franklin Store and five
Reproductions in a yawn. Then replacement
In a shuffle. No one dreams what you've done
Except your friends who now prize duplicates.
They happily steal what they can. But you,
You claw for more. Midnight of no moon and
You slip the junkyard window, shadow against
Shadow in unseeing night, alley dwelling,
Your third arm a crowbar lifted from the
Old Man's shop. Rat feet up rutted asphalt—
No one can detect the Cowboy Kid in this
Dead blackness. Block after block until you're
Behind three stories of 1917 brick and glass.
Your key soothes the pins and with a click and
Muted snap you're inside. Legs of wheat,
You force your way up the stairs and over
Tiles, stench of shaved pencils and ground erasers
Choking you until you reach the office,
Another key twist, and you are there,
File cabinets glowing in the streetlight
Stream through windows. The "S" drawer yields
      like white bread
To the crowbar, and here it is, the Cowboy Kid's
Paperwork—all you've ever wanted from crime.
You collapse in pale blue, the lies and the truth
Typed and scrawled before you. You read: And nothing.
No tears, no slammed fist. Two a.m. when you depart.
Nothing. In daylight, they'll find the file cabinet
Assault behind locked brass. And nothing.
In four years, the umbrella elm out front
      splits in lightning.

Bird Creek Bottom

You saw a man pay six dollars for a pack of Marlboros.
They cost fifty cents at the time you quit during Carter days—
And cheaper still when the Cowboy Kid started swiping Mom's
Bowling alley L&Ms: eleven years old in Bird Creek bottom,
The booty fired by Ohio Blue Tips, tobacco burn
You hated and yearned, down in the dried orange clay,
Johnson grass threats overhanging. You never guessed
Trailer house eyes could betray you. But they did.
And the Old Man scooped you up like a deer carcass
And ass whipped you upside down with a yard dowel.
Then dropped you to the ruined lawn with only this:
    Joe saw you, in the crick bed.

You saw a man pay six dollars—
His skin sun-warped cardboard,
His eyes smashed cherries,
Ears plugged with aids.

You saw a man—

And realized you know him:
He is younger than you.
The Cowboy Kid
Permitted himself
To love only that creek bed
And his dogs. Nothing more.

The dry stream poured nothing into a sudden black jack stand,
Nested with greenbriers and poison ivy, neither tortured you.
You found sandstone slabs long forgotten and wormed your way
Into them, holed up like Bill Doolin and Bill Dalton in an outlaw's lair.
On the coldest days you stripped off your coat and shirt to learn
How much freezing you could stand. You prayed for an L&M but
Denied yourself further theft. The dogs smiled, panting your passion.

One day the Cowboy Kid found a dead cedar branch
And stabbed the dead gray sun. You shouted: *A coyote!*

The woods curled.

Quiet.

Be a Brother

Be a brother, this afternoon and always.

A gray Texaco against a gray highway.
An aluminum day, and the Outlaws
From Oklahoma City shudder aboard,
15 Harley Davidsons and one moon-rumbled
Ancient Indian, parts spanning two decades.
Greasy chains and oiled teeth: remember,
Be a brother. Yawn away any knee collapse.
They align the pump. A splinter called
Weasel manipulates. The pump nozzle is
His sacred nipple: not a drop errs the chapel
Of the gas tanks. Seventy-five cents for the first,
A dollar seven the second. And onward.
A horned toad named Cecil calculates and
Cashiers the due. Everyone pisses, mounts, and
Wheels a thunderstorm into the cooling overcast.
Ears ringing, the Cowboy Kid inspects. Each restroom
Is restaurant neat, save for one greased set of fingers
On the women's room wall. It evaporates
With paper towel effort. After dark, the Cowboy Kid
Latches and then he navigates a Chrysler
To a lightless house that smells of cut sheetrock
And mud. The TV presents *Moby Dick* in Texas
And the Nations—*Red River*, John Wayne every false
Father we've ever known. We pray to Matt
But no one contains that speed. Cycles, cattle, horses
      —all trip your brain.

For reasons deplorable you find yourself in
An earlier place: Cimarron bluffs and hard red dust
And cheap Japanese bikes. Be a brother, you and five others.
Sandstone wheelies and laughter and weed. And then
It is you and two others. Then it is you and motorcycle
Lies and your parents and, finally, a horrid phone call.
In two weeks, you shuffle through hospital control and

See him, the boy you've known longer than any other.
Coma wires, coma tubes, his hair cut back to make him look
As if he's six years old. Six years old—you remember:
Beacon Drive-In and the playground down front, you two,
Red River spread fifty feet above. Now he recedes to
        iodine-stained sheets.

Be a brother, Cowboy Kid, be a brother.

Wind and test pattern howl wring you awake.
Three years have meandered since that gape
In red clay. Even then you understood outlaw karma:
Forty years later and nothing can be roped for good.

Be a brother.

Hopper's Grave

The Cowboy Kid recovers himself while standing
At the foot of Dennis Hopper's grave. In the distance,
Mountains scrape a rain sky. No thunder.
The soil is the color of her hair. Her eyes are
The grass fringe. You compute as you boot-toe
The leavings: twelve plastic motorcycles,
Two dimestore flags (frayed, anemic, blood
Eroded on the Santa Fe plaza), wooden beer crate,
Empty Johnny Walker Red Label fifth. And more:
Cellophane wads, a toy Kansas barn, someone's
Home-broiled film script. You've never been capable
Of explaining how the Cowboy Kid's movie loops
Like fountain water. Child actor in *Have Gun Will Travel*
And *Gunsmoke*. Crowd scenes in three from the Boetticher
Series. Same for *Ride the High Country*. Gawky adolescent
In the bad Duke shows from Mexico, but roping every
Weekend. Mapache soldier in *The Wild Bunch*,
Yet commune spreader in *Easy Rider*. New Buffalo
Cutter-stamped in Malibu Hills. Then, with Dennis
In Peru, suddenly a mature stuntman/rodeo refugee.
Never saw *The Last Movie* debut. Downed in Taos while
Dennis edited a couple of miles away. Studying Zen while
Wearing Levi's, trying to explain the perfect bulldogging run.
The movie is your confrontation, said a master strayed
From San Francisco. (He once published hipster lines.)
Downed later in Red River and Cimarron. Then Greyhound
Windows and reading *Zen and the Art of Motorcycle Maintenance*
On the trail back to Oklahoma. The movie, the confrontation,
None of it real, all of it real as the carved cross
At Dennis' head. She pain wallows miles to the southwest.
The film coils at your chest ignite.

Error Reports on Red Dirt Wrecks

Flash this selfie and the Cowboy Kid glares back.
Your reformat has failed. Corrupted files abound
In those pixels staring back at you, no disk swipe here.
Click and remnants of nights spent beneath
A relay tower, a face fresh-soaped yet already spent,
Listening to Buck Owens and Black Sabbath. Tap and
Recollections of the Let 'R Buck Room in Pendleton
Scroll endlessly. Tap again and tears of four hundred
Women stream from a waterproof case—$37 extra.
Error reports on red dirt wrecks, mescaline bending
Trees and stars and fence posts into one thing.
Explain the logic. Here is a recovered spreadsheet
Of Disciples of Christ training, Reverend Harry Hembree,
Honest and harmless, attempting to shine a light
Against fake wood paneling. Paul & Silas bound in jail,
All night long. Here is Father Joe Thompson texting
Nixon mendacity. But nothing posts. Instead here is
A vid of Bud Lilly's Trout Shop, back when Bud himself
Provided basement instruction, the right bend of the wrist,
Nymph later laid out on the snow-melt brown Yellowstone,
A strike, and your first trout logic poem. True religion here.
True religion newspaper JPG of Hank Williams' last
Lovesick yodel—Skyline Club, December 1952, Austin, Texas,
The Drifter a corpse made up for the public viewing,
No light behind those eyes, voice holy. True religion—
The Skunks at CBGB's or Raul's. Google it and up pops
Charles Plymell's headliner photo of Neal Cassady and
Ann Murphy. Youtube Hank Snow singing "Movin' On."
All of Jimmie Rodgers. Ma Rainey's deep blues moan,
Little Willie John and "You Hurt Me." The Father, Son,
And Merle Haggard of it all—the Gospel according to
St. Thomas and Lightnin' Hopkins. The hard drive failed
When you attempted to webcam God above the sacred mud
Of Blind Willie Johnson in Beaumont. Recovered it reveals
Only Cowboy Don though, beatified virus, sprinkled and

Spring-loaded with the Holy Lone Star, end without world,
    cite this creed.

Cowboy Kid—Cowboy Don's service pack—loops on.

Busted Down

You scramble your knees in live oak shade.
Bud your ears and thunder recedes into
A Terry Allen revue. Ben Johnson is dead
And you're busted down, Cowboy Kid.
The Osage beckons 509 miles away.
Terry Allen sings about suicide by dog leash.
You reply by counting your misgivings:
You never galloped an Appaloosa bareback
Through that tall grass. You never strutted
Buckaroo style. You never stacked dollars
In the oil patch. And yet: This sunset rubs
The color of her nails. You heel dig until
Your back becomes the bark even as acorns
Hail about you. You'd rob a savings-and-loan
For her wind gust. Her eyes outlast polished
Mesquite. Her eyes contract Western Swing
Dancehalls. Her eyes deliver a schottische
At half past midnight as you strain the *charro* line,
But she never stumbles. Her hand on your neck.

You plunge.

She eases your pavement and wind.

Film Work

Perfect preclusion, in free days. David Carradine
All weed and smiles outside his assigned motorhome.
Brenda Vacarro secluded from hidden zoom lenses.
The brick street toasted. The beer joint closed.
For four days you've slotted your time. They have
The Cowboy Kid bibbed and in a newsboy cap.
The job: Explode. You trot beside Carradine's motorcycle.
You arch your cap up two stories. You pound him
On the back through the patchouli smog. Time and again,
Until each cut. Then off to catered salami and your $35 a day.
After shooting one day, Ken Watson calls you to his studio
And posed among the watercolor and acrylic are L.Q. Jones
And R.G. Armstrong. Ken fosters handshakes. Only after you
Leave do you connect them with Peckinpah pictures.
Fast Charlie the Moonbeam Rider is Oklahoma news for a while.
Then, as with all things, it falters: Two years pass before
Its drive-ins only release. The night you saw it, you squinted
Yourself into focus and swallowed forbidden Coors. The next
Days you are cutting class and hitting the pool hall in the
Central State student union basement. You summon War's
"Gypsy Man" from the jukebox and chalk the cue the
Khakied men store behind the counter. Ain't got no home,
Just as the song releases. Try to find your nice young lady,
Someday, but it's a couple of roughnecks drifted in from
West Texas who arrive now. In twenty minutes, they've
Resolved your beer money. You never mentioned that
Sweated preclusion to them. Carradine's name could
Supplant a fist to the mouth—or draw it. Best keep quiet.
You walk out to a gravel and dirt lot. A week earlier, before
Carradine and L.Q. and R.G., you kissed a teacher in a purple
MGB as "Hotel California" debuted on the radio. Her hair was
Amber cashmere. In later years, her son fell to murder—
The Cowboy Kid failing in his own movie.

No Way of Choosing

It slithers into your mind just past an August dawn,
The question that defies parking garage enforcement.
You fall against an elevator wall. Cement sweat invades
Your clothes. In the hard summer sun angle you
Acknowledge: Rodeo girls bore little in the way
Of choosing back then. B&W images of charcoal
Hats with crisp brims. Cuffed Wranglers over bottom-line
Boots. Belt tooled by the drunk living in the sandstone
Lumber mill out by the railroad tracks (soon to meet his end
Beneath those steel wheels). Backseats, pickup beds,
A frame house—the surrender is always identical, quick
And threatening. Ribbon roping and record dancing,
Then the missing: a cowboy lost on a highway, *gone,*
Dependable calendar days, *gone.* No money, unlike
The bank daughters, the tool-pusher daughters.

No way of choosing. . .

So we're left with phone calls unanswered at Texas arenas,
Unwritten letters, and a need to fashion the untrue into a
Baggy thick coat to be worn for generations. Only one road:
Carry it forward. But you are wracked by this wondering,
The Cowboy Kid pinned to the concrete.

If laws had been different back then. . .

You wonder but the answer is hard as this wall:
The Cowboy Kid forsakes his layer of wind.

PG&BTK Redux

The movie suspends for the sixth time.
Here is Slim Pickens, gut shot. He oozes
All that he is or ever will be into the creek
Before him. He is positioned between
Two thief-less trees. His mask is Durango
Agony, Durango acceptance. Time to commit
His *pistolas* to the clay. Death-smears hang gray
Around him, but the stream carries him toward
One spool-head of light and elevation. All things are
Completed. Here is Katy Jurado captured in
Fourteenth century Spanish oils. No face like hers:
Blasted, weeping, smiling at once: the awful pain
Of desire (with Dylan hums in the background).
The Cowboy Kid becomes his Melba seat yet again
And understands. Here he is in dust and splendor.
Two minutes of forever consumes. Slim & Katy,
Katy & Slim. And still the creek flows. You exit this
Moment, and a life beyond has shifted nowhere.

Racing

I motored around Denton one Christmas
Alone as usual through the slate noon—
Still listening to radio back then
And Joni Mitchell's "Song for Sharon" filled
My cheap speakers—only time I ever
Heard it on the road. My brother was dead,
My marriage was done, and I knew one thing:

I would push love onto the service road
And race away as fast as I could. Always.

Sam Shepard Ate Posole

Sam Shepard ate posole and tortillas at the next table.
I borrowed his mail. March snow littered the plaza.
No one cared.
I read about broken sidewalks and cracked hearts.
Some evenings I worked Upstart Crows, patio moist,
         watching for the Lord.
Years earlier I read my own weavings at St. Mark's.
Now I sit in wheelchair Oklahoma.
The gray dies.
Two friends once wore Osage locks and faced the La Fonda.
Pendleton blankets cocooned their torsos.
Tourists snapped them with 1973 Yashicas.
Santa Fe cops kept their paces.
I saw Sam Shepard stroll the plaza with a walking stick
         straight from Woolworth's.
He roamed wide back then.
Patti Smith lines rhymed his pockets.
We had to leave early for Pawhuska—allottee funeral.
I lost my way past the peyote church.
Another time, near Deming, I streamed a bar.
I fell down the open door.
A brakeless wood truck slipped me by inches.
I never drank again.
Sam Shepard was a movie star by then.
Letters lent cannot be returned.
We paste them upside down between boards.
We granite pound them and apologize for nothing.
My eyes open three hours before dawn today.
Sam Shepard is the snow owl in the lean-to.

Standing on Sam Bass

The world is bobbing around.
You get that now as you lean against
A monument too ugly for souvenirs.
The real stone is beheaded.
The real stone rests among library books,
        free of chippers.
The real stone bled out beyond chalk doors
Where you sipped coffee during wet breeze days.
But it is July now—grasshopper hours and less—
Today is one hundred thirty-five years
        down some broken line:
And you'll pick up the iron, pick up the powder,
And breathe the fire.
Or you're nothing at all.

Sam Bass is caliche clawing your boots.
He is Bible brimstone carvings.
He is the last white man before slave
        and freedman territory
Here in a far corner of this burying soil.
Sam Bass is a cedar waxwing displaced
In dead live oaks. He is the mahogany
Wasp hunting in tombstone grass.
The collapsed trailer house beyond
Graveyard fences—
That is Sam Bass too.

He expanded into these things
As they dragged his box behind two mules:
A Methodist preacher self-shamed into words,
A lost head in a cotton patch shaking no,
A July rider on a big bay dismounted
        to throw an anger clod

At a fresh death mound,
No one strutting to confront him.

Standing on Sam Bass
You stare through open hands
At the horseman who escaped Old Town
        into Brushy Creek
Always to resurrect
Blood on scalloped skies.

Tonight You Wish You Knew Willie

i.

Tonight you wish you knew Willie well enough
       To stop by Pedernales and complain
       About Austin's ruined skyline and confess
       Your woman vexation and withered parent views
       And work dread and Zen catastrophe.

You sleep with Geronimo tattooed above your pillows.
Willie would applaud that devotion.

You wish you knew Willie so you could share your chants
       And shopping lists and ask how he stopped
       Writing songs and what to do about slices and toe shots
       And explain you're infected by Django too.

You want to walk tilted floors with Willie while there's time.

Tonight you wish you knew Willie well enough
       To tell him how drought squeezed you
       And how too often you feel wood solemn.
       You want to talk about Longhorn football—
       How perfect it was, those fifty-yard-line seats
       In an October Cotton Bowl, 1976, and the Tyler Rose—
Back when *Red Headed Stranger* still pumped tears.

Nothing's been right since.

Did he ride with Geronimo a lifetime or more ago?
How much Torreón mescal did he inhale with Peckinpah?
Has he straddled a vintage Indian motorcycle?
Does he still own Charlie Dunn boots?
Did he bust down your fence and gate in a restored
       International Harvester Scout
To mud mummy-dry upper Barton Creek?

They say he sometimes requires a leaning shoulder to walk
      these days.

Tonight you wish you could roll out biscuit dough
      And roll up spliffs stout enough
      To coax rust from barbed wire, smooth enough
      To dispatch invading cedars to Oklahoma
      And, stoned, you and Willie would eat
      Mountain honey and praise Floyd Tillman
And confess to a kind of holy roller reincarnation.

You wish you knew Shotgun Willie well enough
      To explain how you slipped back to imagination
      After two days in the Piedras Negras lockup
      For rurales lies—and walked when by rights
      You should have floated the river.
      No dream could have bettered that.

ii.

But tonight Willie sings in Ireland.
Or someplace.

For you, tonight is a sticky black room.
It stinks of rodeo ammonia.
Thunder pounds distant country.
But here no rains splash.
Here truck drivers moan through walls.
Here Interstates beckon no one.
Geronimo is a century dead and more.

Willie? You saw him once at a funeral.
You nodded. He nodded back.
No words bartered.

Years ago you sank in a stolen pool.
Mahogany wasps lit to sip near your nose.

You freed yourself from the movie then.
You peaked a mountain, in that deep water.

You were.

Tequila Nonsense

No sotol on the shelf so I bought
A dusty fifth of tequila and drove
Toward Marathon, just one stop along
The way, the sky oozing purple
And red along the horizon until
Somewhere around Sanderson.
I found a place to park for the night
And broke the seal, the first fiery
Swallow dropping deep into my boots.
I leaned back against the stars and peeled
José Cuervo's name from the bottle,
Then drank more. I felt Jalisco
Swim through my blood and brooded:

If I had to do it over, I'd build a house
Of caliche, curse the rain, praise the wind,
And sing of los mesteños, ride like lightning—
Never fall to a woman, never own a credit card,
And proclaim: I refuse to bend to this age!

But then I reined myself:
Enough tequila nonsense.
I threw the bottle into
The dark-frustrated guajillos.

Trudging After Joe Frazier

You tussle with iced-down shadows,
Each step echo lost in the breath
Bursts of five a.m. solitude.
You crave bed warmth and locked windows—
But Joe Frazier never needed anything easy.
Joe Frazier never caught a break and wanted
        it that way.

We have a saying in this brotherhood:
I'm going to put my head on your chest.
It means I'm going to take your best
And climb right through it to your heart,
The more you throw, the better for me.
Joe Frazier could push it to the axe edge
        of dying.

So here you are in the pre-dawn frost,
Measuring your lost prophecies against
The fuel of a 1971 fight in the Garden—
You're not much, boy, face it:
You couldn't make it a minute of round one.
Yet you trudge after Frazier, vain to breathe
A whiff of what spun the century
When the world could still be floored.

Waylon and Pinball

Flood fouled Saturday
And I fall into a trailer court
East of Guthrie, Oklahoma—
A Pinto ride removed
From Barbara Barnes bliss:

I wait with her brother.

Houses of the Holy rumble
On high-fi I could never afford—
He has a bong four feet long
And I lose my legs on Thai weed
And hopeless 3.2 beer fumes:

I'm cemented to this mobile home.

Yet I eventually manage to rise
Folding Zeppelin "No Quarter"
And pill bug myself to that Pinto—
Roll all the way to Kingfisher
Red gray mud water wings
A foot beyond my howling ears:

We pass the reincarnation dance hall.

Sandstone truck stop black bus idle
But no Barbara Barnes—instead
Six feet of country singer with devil
        whiskers
Coal hat, darker eyes summoning—
C'mon, hoss, quarter a game?

Pinball is what he had in mind
And he guards the Joker's Wild
And, *why the hell not?*

He rests the legs on his toes
To slow the ball:

I know I'm in trouble for sure.

He nods toward the next machine—
The single-play Bowl-A-Strike—
Without taking his eyes from
His joker's bumpers
And I drop my dime to flashing rings:

Begin.

For two hours we go—
Waylon and I
Marlboros pasted to our lips
Truck drivers inching up
Around us, coveralls dripping
Sinclair-brand grease:

How much of your life have you
        wasted on that Led Zeppelin shit?

Waylon asks that as he inches
His steel orb through a triple-score
Alighting another extra ball—
Ain't won you much in the way
Of pussy or dollar bills, has it?
I lean in and TILT the Bowl-A-Strike:

My ball descends through the dead machine.

Waylon laughs and counts up
The quarters I owe him—
Don't fret, hoss, most guys
Never have the chance to learn this
        lesson—

And he and the Waylors load the bus
Lonesome, ornery, and mean:

They howl away, black through rain.

I bear my lifeless ball outside
Nothing but frozen flippers
And bumpers unyielding—
Rusted plunger, busted
Kickers and slingshots
Filled holes, sprung saucers
Missing switches and gates
Magic posts all bent—
Rain on the glass above:

I chase after Waylon, leaving
Barbara Barnes and Pintos behind—
Making the run up the ramp rewarding:

FREE GAME.

Cinnamon Shadows

Welcome to these cinnamon shadows:
Mary Beth's hair pure as the night
With a shimmer drawing you to those
Highland Maui pot ranches she left behind—
And she's a horsewoman too,
Rides the saddle as easily as she smiles.
She matches everything.

She has no clue
You keep a .38 Smith & Wesson
        beneath the seat.
She heard you wrote poems.
She trusted your hair.
She has no clue.

Tonight—no advantage of any kind.
Tonight— pizza and falling talk.
Tonight— FM radio, no pretense.
Then the news interruption:

Convair CV-300 forest crash
You rise from the innocent bed,
Darkness over darkness—
Death of the barefoot songster.

"You like those guys?" she said.
Much as you love your revolver,
But you can't say those words.
You walk the room, understanding
You'll never know that touch again.
Shirtless in Levi's you head outside—
Wood rotted porch, the whole house
To be bulldozed in three months—
Safeway parking lot expansion.

I like those guys,
You say to the 1977 blank sky.

Tex Cobb

You never fall.
You take and give
And take and take.
You never fall.

Sometimes Philadelphia
Is the Australian Outback:
No place is better
To be alone in wilderness.

Sometimes the rainbow
Of bruised flesh
Is a beautiful thing
Below a Western hat.

Sometimes the loser
Beats the winner
To the post-fight
Cocktail party.

You laugh and say
Let's do it again, I'm ready,
And we love the loser
More than the champ.

Sometimes you say Christ
Means more than Christianity.
Sometimes you're Buddha
Behind destroyed flesh.

No one understands
Why you cannot fall.
Standing is Nirvana.
Standing is payday.

Sometimes in Philadelphia
We need a cowboy.
Sometimes on TV
We need you on your feet.

All us who fail ourselves,
        we need you.
Walk well in the wilderness.
Follow Jesus and Hank.
We need you.

I Wore a Hank Williams T-Shirt

I wore a Hank Williams t-shirt the day
I retrieved my father's cremains. Portland
In August but the wind nearly froze me
Up on Pill Hill. The pathologist spoke:
These are not ashes—this is a mineral box.
It will be heavier than you think.
I carried my father's weight through the ice
Of a sunny day, med students smiling,
Maybe at the paper-wrapped cardboard,
   Maybe at Hank.
I wore the same Hank Williams t-shirt
The day I drove down to Turner.
I parked the Nissan rental beyond a tavern
Then soaked in acclaim as I stepped inside:
   Great t-shirt! Great t-shirt!
I drank an Olympia. My father preferred Coors—
I knew that story. He was a Colorado cowboy.
(After they freed him from jail in Oakland,
He bought cases of Coors for the pickup's
Front seat. The bed glittered gold beer cans
By the time he reached Beaverton's shadows. . .)
Hank Williams guided me from the tavern
And I drove drunken asphalt to the barn.
The Winnebago reclined on concrete blocks
While a chained goat slept in doghouse shade.
Your daddy sure could have used you back then.
I breathed whiskey and rust in that dead motor home.
   I required air.
The white haired man who knew my father
Hitched me to blackberry ditches and firs.
We sang as one: Hank Williams' "Ramblin' Man."
But nothing could join us.

I Wore a Paris, Texas, T-Shirt

I wore a *Paris, Texas* t-shirt
To the class reunion. Two people

Died in a head-on crash on
Gar Creek Bridge—we worried

We possessed their souls. But they were
Strangers and we sighed as helicopters

Levitated bodies to an earthquake night.
People I should have recognized

Fingered Nastassja and Harry Dean
On my chest, asking, "Who are they?"

"The people in the wreck," I said.
My classmates climbed away from me.

I ached for Texas.

A black guy with a shaved head
Stepped outside with me.

We fired some weed before it rained.
"High school shit never crumbles,"

He said, and I nodded. Red and
Blue flashes still pulsed the night.

Women I knew as girls line-danced
Inside. Their husbands watched OU

Football in the bar. Everyone was
Gray and crumpled. No one felt

Distinguished. My best friend from

High school flew to Louisville

Instead of showing up for this.
I was happy to be stoned.

Nastassja and Harry Dean
Joined me at the wall

Where deceased classmates
Stared at refreshments.

We studied those photos
From 1974—only the dead

Remain forever young.
The disk jockey played

"Long May You Run."
People demanded disco.

It was time to leave.

Outside my boots carried
Me to the fatality scrap

Above Gar Creek. I slid
On glass shatter and chrome.

No one saw us hurdle the rail:
Nastassja, Harry Dean, and me.

We became gator-toothed
Fish in that slime water—

Fierce to be lost and forgotten.

I Wore a Charles Plymell T-Shirt

I wore a Charles Plymell T-shirt—
Panik In Dodge City—
To the nursing home. The old man
Had turned the color of raw shrimp.
He groaned and tottered an arm.
He feared window blinds.

No one else wore cowboy boots.
No one else wore ragged Levi's.
No one else wore a Mexican belt.
I was the only one.

You don't know how bad it is, he said.
The old man's voice belonged
       to someone else.
You ache like Texas, he said.
I can never make it to the kitchen, he said.

He closed his eyes. I walked outside.
I swallowed sunshine and rubbed
Wheat sky on my Charles Plymell t-shirt.
Every day is good for dying.

For a moment I slid off to harrowed fields
And bloodied dirt devils and Charley riding
In a tractor baby box. You still found
Open range in western Oklahoma
       back then.
You could ride a horse to Hollywood
And never fight highway or fence.

Those times invented the old man
But never totaled anything for him.
He came up lost.

You don't crane in boots and Mexican belt

For too long in land now foreign to you.
I peered down the nursing home ridge
Then took off in a blue automobile
        praying to saddle and bridle.

I wore a Charles Plymell t-shirt.
It kept me breathing.

Wichita Lineman

i.

And it is forever the same:
Here is an Interstate highway,
Spoiled biscuit dough slush
Threatening the right-of-way.

Here are a mother and son
Navigating bad asphalt
In a new Chevy Caprice wagon—
Fake wood side panels.

Here are pickups and horse trailers,
Eighteen-wheel fuel tankers,
Cowboy hitch-hikers frozen
In hammered rough-out boots.

And it is forever the same...

That song on the radio,
Four months old but new,
Declares everything you can know
From the Caprice dashboard.

That country:
Endless poles and lines
And fences ice-wrapped
Between bois d'arc corners—

Sky and plains as one
Gray as this ruined sludge,
Promising nothing—
And it is forever the same.

ii.

Parking garage, Oklahoma City,
Packing Town stench today,
Will Rogers World Airport,
Named for a man snuffed in frost and fire.

1969 and Nixon is new:
Young men in Vietnam green
Hustle duffle bags to waiting
Fords and Oldsmobiles.

Can we wait until the song is over?
And you absorb that fade-out jangle:
Always this will be your airport song,
Always need and want will stretch away

Like telephone wires,
Like rising airliners.

iii.

Sleet ignites your face
As you cross to the terminal—
You enter at the moment to hear
The flight is hidden behind time.

So: you wait.
Mom brought one of her "books"—
The new *Ladies Home Journal*—
You are free to stampede:

The restrooms where stalls demand a dime.
The TV chairs that cost a quarter for B&W.
The off-limits bar/private club where men
With whiskey skin dissolve into wallpaper.

You hit the fake tower
And slide a nickel into a telescope
To watch TWA and Continental
Going nowhere.

He gave you The White Album
Before he left for San Diego, M.C.R.D.—
Cellophane removed so he could see
What was hidden inside, he said—

In fact, he bought it for himself,
Took a listen or two,
Decided he despised it,
Dumped it on you.

You know that now.
You know as you watch
Dead airplanes
In the sleet.

The pay telescope clicks black.

iv.

Mom snores beneath her *Journal.*
You sit and stare, nickels burned.
A hippie girl is your salvation
But it won't happen today—

Everything is coats and boots and hats.
Everyone is miles away walking past.
Everything is everyone and weary when
You hear the flight number announced.

You wake her and hurry down the corridors
To the pre-terrorist gates and elbow
Your position—he is the last off the plane:
Marine khaki, Marine bald, no eyes.

His duffle bag is road kill.

In the car he Zippos a Camel
And speaks boot camp boasts.
But soon the cigarette joins the slush
And he snores like passing diesels.

Mom stares straight at nothing.
You fall deeper than the backseat,
No White Album puzzles corrected—
And it is forever the same.

Glen Campbell returns to the speaker
At just the right moment:
The stretch down south somehow holds the strain
With voice and guitar and Oklahoma words.

Only then the entirety of it concedes—
A line of blue sketches in the west.

Part II: Dying in Red Dirt Country

Dying in Red Dirt Country

1.

He's dying up there in red dirt country.

Some days, he's addled in a bed, muttering threats about leaving the kitchen though he's nowhere near a kitchen. His sense of reason expires with the sunset. He frightens the people exposed to him. Then, a few days later, he'll be on the phone to me, expressing his shock when he learns of what he said when he was out of his mind. "I'm just so confused by it," he says. Then a couple of days after that, he's back outside on his rusted Ford tractor, battling Johnson grass, the only enemy left for him from his lifelong wars. (The other foes—busted up cars, undrilled oil wells, fracking trucks, cattle, meadows dotted with unhauled hay bales, crooked county politicians, stubborn teams of mules and horses—retreated long ago.) Awhile back, the tractor broke down in the far corner of his acreage on my home town's east edge. Too crippled to walk any distance, he crawled a quarter of a mile back to the house.

He's dying, and at four score and more years, he's entitled to move on to whatever is next. But I can't get my arms around it. It's easier for me to conceive of the Gulf of Mexico drying up.

89

2

Here are some words: hate, fear, outrage, shame, insecurity, cruelty. Disloyalty, disrespect. Disconnected. Denial. Paradox and hypocrisy. Failure. Sorrow.

Brutality.

And love—eventually, of a sort.

And debt—one that went unrecognized for too long.

You can apply those words to me and my stepfather, and aspects of our relationship over the years, although, at times, when I was young, it was hardly a relationship at all. But those words are mostly abstractions that I don't trust. One rainy noon, years after I'd fled Oklahoma for Austin, Texas, I found myself sitting in a psychologist's office, staring out at weather-paralyzed traffic on Mopac Expressway. I was not sure why I was there, not exactly. The psychologist asked a couple of questions about my childhood and about a stepbrother I'd mentioned, who'd died young. Suddenly I found myself with tears on my cheeks. It wasn't as bad as what a lot of people went through, I heard myself say about my childhood.

"Things can be subtly horrific," the psychologist said.

No, no—there was nothing subtle about it. Subtlety would actually have been a delightful change. Everything concerning my home-life as a kid was loud, full-bore, over-the-top, and punctuated by farts, burps, and hawked up spit.

What I was trying to tell the psychologist was this: the story of the old man is not one of Drunk Dad. For years after he became my stepdad, he had a taste for cheap Falstaff beer and, when he felt like splurging, Coors—then the sanctified beer of the West, a delicacy unknown to philistines east of the Mississippi. Whiskey was always in the places where we lived: Old Forester, usually; sometimes, Calvert. In the 1960s, Griffin's strawberry preserves, produced in Muskogee, Oklahoma, came in wide-mouthed glass containers with tin lids you pried open with the blunt end of a church key. When empty, these containers became our drinking glasses (I don't remember us having store-bought glassware), and the old man would stir up frothy mixtures of Coke and whiskey to gulp. But I can recall seeing him drunk no more than three or four times over the course of more than a half-century. And he was a pleasant drunk.

He was not Gambler Dad, either. He nickeled and dimed with the other men at my home town's four-lane bowling alley—the only "sport" he participated in—and he might have played a few hands of pitch or dominoes at a penny a point, but that would have been the full extent of his gaming. And he was not Pervert Dad. To be sure, he married his first wife when she was a teenager and he was twenty-two, but that was not uncommon in places like my hometown at the time they came together. He and my mother had frequent sex. I know because we lived, at first, in a tiny trailer and, then, in two small houses in which the sounds of their amorous undertakings could not be muffled. Aside from that, he was something of a prude. I'm confident he never strayed once he married my mother, never was tempted. He never explained the birds and bees to me (no one did—I learned those lessons from my stepbrother's hidden stash of Playboys); my guess is that he would have been confused and embarrassed by attempting to do so.

We had just two conversations during my whole life that concerned sex even peripherally. The first was an admonition: never take a job at a local funeral home owned by a long-dead man, who was, the old man said, notorious for "aiming young men toward the queer." The second was just a passing comment about his first father-in-law, the town's police chief, who found himself in trouble with the mayor and city council for sporting with too many of the wrong sort of married women. The only time I ever saw the old man disgusted with himself was immediately after he mentioned these things to me.

So what is this—Dad's story? He's dying up there in red dirt country—and I don't know how to render him with a simple phrase.

3.

We drove all across southwest Oklahoma and down into Texas in a 1948 Ford pickup. Going to make some big money in the oil boom out there. Oh yeah. Weren't no interstates in them days, of course. Hell, you was doing good to find a two-lane with a shoulder on it. We took turns driving, and you tried to sleep on the passenger's side in the cab when you wasn't driving. Or maybe you even tried stretching out in the bed. But it wasn't no good. Damned old pickup was rough as a cob to ride in. We was about wore out by the time we got to Snyder. This must have been 1949. We pulled up to this café because we was about half-starved by then. We no sooner climbed out of the truck than these two Mexicans come flying out the café's door, going at each other with knives. They bloodied each other up pretty good in a hurry. I mean, they was really going at it. Just a couple of minutes later, a Snyder policeman rolled up and stepped out of his car and, calm as could be, pulled his pistol and shot both of those Mexicans. Just like that. Never done anything to that cop for shooting them.

Well, big money. We got jobs roughnecking morning tower, and we found a place to live, just this little dinky old trailer. And we had to pay about what we made roughnecking just to rent it. Hell, everything was jacked up. You had to pay a dollar for a single egg at the grocery store. That's how it was.

Everything was fixed, and the town was wide open. Their little old jail couldn't hold everyone, so they went up and cut down a bunch of cottonwood logs from along the Colorado River north of Snyder, built this kind of stockade. If you was drunk or fighting or whatever, they'd pick you up and lock you in that pen and hold you there until the company you worked for sent some men down with the money to bail you out so you could go to work. Yeah, that's how it was. One time we come home from the rig to find the trailer had been broke in to. All our tools had been stole. We talked to a Snyder cop, and he pretty much just laughed in our faces. . . .

4

My "real" father straddled the line between rodeo cowboy and carnie. He was long gone before I drew my first breath, and I never caught up with him until he was a box of ashes. I lived with my mother at my grandparents' house on the west hill the first three years of my life.

Peggy's house was next door. Peggy and her daughters had no telephone, so they borrowed by grandparents' party line. We'd hand the receiver to them through the dining room window. They also lacked indoor plumbing. From that same dining room window, I'd watch them walk from their back door to the outhouse by the alley. Mr. Daniels, who lived across the alley from my grandparents, also had an outhouse. He was diabetic, and he taught my uncles how to give him injections of insulin with the foulest looking syringe I've ever seen. Mr. Daniels went missing for a few days, and Grandpa went looking for him. He found him dead in the outhouse, his overalls down around his ankles. My grandparents had indoor plumbing. Grandpa dug the trench for the sewer line by hand, using just a shovel. He did the work every night after supper, after he'd come home from his job as a mechanic at the Studebaker garage. This happened before I was born. Grandpa knocked down the old outhouse and filled in the pit with dirt. A healthy apricot tree was growing in its place by the time my memories began.

I had no baby bed. I slept on a couch with dining room chairs backed up to it to keep me from rolling off. I say couch. It was not called a couch. It was called a divan. It wasn't, strictly speaking, a divan. But in that time and place, divan was the word used instead of couch or sofa. And we called lunch "dinner" and dinner "supper." And ain't was a perfectly acceptable contraction. A creek was a "crick." A wren, a "ray-un." The viaduct that connected the west and east sides of town was a "vie-dock." Vienna sausages were "vee-nee sausages." The street out front was not paved, and there was a horse lot beyond the Johnson-grass-choked bar-ditch. The wind really does come sweeping down the plain up there, and red dirt dust swirled constantly. The house grew ice-house cold on winter nights. Around 5:30, Grandpa made the round of wall-mounted gas stoves with a box of Ohio Blue Tip matches, and the gradual spreading of warmth is the most reassuring thing I've ever felt.

I loved that house and those people.

I loved the few toys I had and the toy metal barn I had.

I did not love it when, one night, my mother awakened me to introduce me to a bald man with huge arms and hands, who tried shaking me around a little while he laughed and laughed as a way to convince me I should like him.

A few weeks later, the bald man returned with his sons, four and a half and five and a half years older than I. Within a half-hour, they broke most of my toys and stomped my toy metal barn flat. I did not love that, either.

5.

The old man and Mom ran off to Judge Slammin' Sam Sullivan's marriage factory in Durant, Oklahoma. Durant sits hard on the shores of Lake Texoma, and in those days, it catered to elopers. Twenty-four/seven, you could show up in town with a handful of cash, get a marriage license, get the required blood test to prove you didn't have syphilis, and then get hitched by Judge Sam. After which you could run off to enjoy honeymoon bliss at one of the vacation courts out by the muddy reservoir. The whole operation was set up primarily to service Texas teenagers attempting to tie the knot before their parents could intervene, Oklahoma's age of consent being roughly the same as Shakespeare's Verona.

Shortly after they returned from Durant, we moved into an ABC trailer house situated adjacent to the old man's auto repair shop, which, in turn, was in the back yard of his mother's place. The trailer house measured 10 x 50—five hundred square feet. Five of us lived there—Mom, the old man, his two sons, me.

I hated it from the beginning.

6.

You might say Dee Freeman was a wholesaler. He wasn't much interested in selling just a bottle or two at a time. You could buy a bottle at several places around town, like one of the pool halls. Or at Rick's place—Rick usually had a bottle or two he'd sell you. And there was a nigger named Spoon who had a shoeshine parlor where he sold moonshine, but we're talking about bonded whiskey. Dee sold by the case to these other places. Well, we worked on his cars. You could take a '48 Ford and soup it up and put what you might say were special springs on it, and then you could fit twenty cases of whiskey in it. Oh, yeah, a Hudson Hornet was a bootlegger's dream, but the highway patrol was always on the lookout for them. But a Ford? Naw, they was too many of them. Dee and me had talked a lot. He explained about how if the highway patrol got onto you, you just left the highway and got onto one of them dirt county roads, and you just turned the steering wheel from side to side so that you'd kick up as much red dirt as you could. And pretty soon that trooper behind you wouldn't be able to tell if he was coming or going. And you'd slip over onto another road at an intersection then make your way back onto the highway while the trooper was going around in circles on the county roads.

Oh, I was going to be a big shot. I had it figured that driving one run down to Fort Worth and back for Dee, I could make about as much as I could in a month working at the Ford garage. Well, my dad got wind of what I was thinking, and he put a stop to that in a hurry, let me tell you.

Dee had an upstairs apartment on Harrison Avenue, right across from the newspaper office. I was there one night, having a drink and just talking, when the police come busting in. They'd raid him a couple of times a year, then Dee'd pay everyone off and the whole thing would be forgotten until it was time for the next raid. So Dee says to these cops, "You stay right where you are." He points at me, then says, "This young man ain't got nothing to do with any of this. You're going to let him walk down the back stairs so he can go home. Then you can come in, and we'll settle this thing." Well, the cops done just that. That's how Dee was. Come election time, he'd pay the rent so the Democrats could have their county headquarters, and he'd pay the rent so the Republicans could have their county headquarters. . . .

7.

Tonight, the call comes at a time of failed rain and soulless skies. He has fallen off his chair. A trip to the emergency room, a round of painkillers, and he's back in his darkened lair. His mind has rushed away to that other place. The house is full of cats. What are they going to do about all these cats? Too many cats crowd his bed. Where is he supposed to sleep with all those cats on his mattress?

Mom's last cat died maybe twenty years ago.

Honey, she says, there are no cats. The only thing on your bed are pillows.

That expression she hates to see descends on his face as some part of his mind accepts that what she says is correct and he wonders how he could have been so wrong—even while his brain conjures another delusion.

8.

I hated him from the beginning. I'm ashamed to say it, but it's true. I never gave him a chance.

Many, many years later, we sat talking in a dark living room. He was holding forth on the relationship between parents and children. "You have a favorite," he said. "It don't really do any good to pretend otherwise." My oldest stepbrother was clearly the favorite, then and now. My other stepbrother was a distant second. Me? I failed even to place or show. I was there because there was nothing else to do with me. I was attached to the prize that was my mother. Or that's how I saw it as a kid. Now I know it was more complicated.

The old man loved any dessert with pineapple in it. I loathed pineapple.

The old man reviled grape jelly. It became my favorite.

And on it went.

Once, Mom came down with a "sick headache" that left her bed-ridden. Or maybe it was a kidney infection. She suffered both. Whatever the case, she was too sick to make supper, so the old man cooked for us three boys. When he turned his back, I scraped my food into a nearby trashcan. He was not fooled. He found the found food, dug it out of the trash, shoved it into my mouth, and held my nose until I swallowed. He also made me eat garbage, coffee grounds, and eggshells while he was at it. My stepbrothers laughed. The old man got on to them for it, but they continued to giggle under their breath. Leave It to Beaver and The Adventures of Ozzie and Harriet came on TV. I'd watch those shows on the B&W set in the living room with my stepbrothers and parents. I didn't understand. They were science fiction.

9

The meds don't take. One morning, he can't get out of bed. Blisters the size of beer bottle caps erupt on his legs. His legs themselves are red as an autumn dawn and swollen to nearly twice their normal size. He's had a dead eye for most of his life. Cataracts and glaucoma have now savaged his good one. In recent years, he's moved through a reality of haze and rain-bleary windows. This morning, he can't see at all. This morning, he's supposed to enter hospice. But he can't even get out of bed. The home health nurse who visits immediately calls his doctor. The doctors says to take him to the ER. Before noon, he's in ICU.

Can't even get out of bed.

It's inconceivable. I used to tell people if they wanted to get an image of pure testosterone, they need only look at him. Bald—yes, but not in the usual way. When he was in his twenties, a water heater pilot light ignited a gasoline tank, and a wad of fire seared the hair from his head. No hospital for him. No, he drove himself to the doctor's office. The doctor told him to spray his head with Foille, a canned burn treatment that smelled like horse puke. He took the rest of the day off, then headed back to work. For weeks after that, he'd rub his scalp and hunks of flesh would just come off on his fingers.

For a while, he worked on county-owned trucks at his garage. (That came to an end when a county commissioner showed up at the shop one day, asking for a kickback for the work the old man performed on the commissioner's road crew vehicles. The old man told him where to stick it.) One afternoon, I watched a county dump truck tow another dump truck to the gravel and oil-encrusted lot outside the north door to the shop. The county boys left the stricken truck there and drove away. The old man disconnected the driveshaft then wrapped a chain around the truck's grille. He looped the chain over his shoulder and dragged the dump truck into his shop, his legs working the concrete like a Clydesdale's. I've never seen anything like it since that day. It made the beef-cases on the cable TV tough-man contests look like pansies.

He was strong. He had cantaloupe biceps and cantaloupe calves and an ass as flat as a brick. He was barrel chested, and while he always sported a gut, the proportion of muscle to fat made it seem insignificant. Yes, he was strong, but beyond that, he was tough. I learned the difference from hanging out with bull riders and boxers. Anyone can get strong, but toughness comes from doing battle with the world and scarring over and forcing yourself to keep going, never mind cracked bones and torn tissue and loosened teeth. I would say the old man's hands were steer hide, but that seems too soft. Years of battling chains and wrench handles and sledgehammers and white hot exhaust pipes and spewing radiators had rendered them into giant calluses, permanently blackened by oil and grime. His nails were like ugly yellow slices of stone pounded into place.

One day, we were getting ready to drag a trailer house over two hundred miles of two-lane behind a homemade tow truck. Something about the hitch didn't suit him. He spread a cloth fender cover on the gravel and red dirt beneath the rear end of that old Ford, then wheeled his cutting torch out of the shop. He lit the torch, pulled on some goggles, and crawled under the truck. Sparks rained on him as he worked, landing on his bare hands and face, his coveralls, the fender cover. After a moment or two, the fender cover caught fire. Flames burned toward his head. I waved my arms at him and pointed. He saw me, glanced at the flames, then gave me a look of total disgust, and went back to cutting metal. He finished his job just as the fire was reaching his ear. He calmly reached over with one of his bare hands, wadded up the burning cloth, and then slapped it a couple of times until the flames were gone. He shot me that look again: you're the most pathetic wimp in the world. Then, he crawled out from under the Ford.

He was stocky. I was lean. He was hairy as a squirrel. I had little body hair and, later, a light beard. He was fair-skinned and, for all his battle-hardened skin, could sunburn easily. I turned the color of a pecan when warm weather rolled around—Mom always said this was because I was part American Indian through her father (a DNA test years later proved this to be untrue). The old man and his boys were circumcised. I was, in the parlance of these times, uncut. But above all else, I was lacking in toughness.

Today, I spent two hours in a boxing gym, part of the time training with a retired pro who had more than twenty fights on his record. Today, the old man can't get out of bed. Yet, I still think I come up short by his standards.

I'll always feel that way. I've never dragged a dump truck into a shop.

10.

I remember the '30s. God a'Friday, you don't get over something like that. They say we wasn't in the Dust Bowl exactly—that was farther west. Well, that may be, but I can tell you I saw that dirt blow in. It grew in the sky like a thunderstorm—only it was what you might call red-brown. You could taste it first before it ever got here. Then you smelled it. You tried to get the stock in the barn and the chickens in the henhouse on account of they couldn't survive it. Them old cows would get down with dust and couldn't get up, and they'd just die right there in the pasture. Then you tried to lock yourself up in the house. Of course, houses wasn't tight as they are now, but you shut them up as best you could. Mother would hang wet sheets over the windows. And you stuffed wet towels in cracks. Anything you could do. Then the storm would hit, and, buddy, let me tell you, it was just like a damned thunderstorm rolling through. It was a loud rumble. But not a drop of rain, of course. And you'd put handkerchiefs over your mouth and nose, but nothing really helped. Then it would end, and the house would be plain filthy. Many's the time I saw Mother clean up the floors with a scoop shovel.

And the heat! I'll never forget the summer of '36. Good God, it was a hundred, a hundred and five, sometimes over a hundred and ten, day after day after day. Everything burned up. There was no air-conditioning, no water coolers, nothing. We didn't even have a fan. You'd open the windows, and half the time, there wouldn't be no breeze, or if there was, it'd be hotter than the inside of the house. Me and my brothers, we hammered together what you might say was a kind of raft, and there was one pond on the place, and it had a little spring that fed it. We put that raft in it, and at the end of the day, after we was done with chores, we'd go down there and strip off and get in the water and just kind of hang on to it. That was the only cool we got.

Dad was working in town at the Ford garage, and I'd help him out some—I was just a kid, after school, didn't get paid nothing for it. The stadium wasn't built yet, that come with the W.P.A., and there was just a big kind of gully, you might say, over there south of Harrison Avenue with a kind of swinging bridge for the sidewalk. There was this man come through one time, and he was from out of town, and he wasn't dressed in overalls or nothing, but done up pretty nice in a suit and tie. So he had some money, and no one had any money then. I saw him as I walked over that bridge on the way to the garage. He seemed pretty much in a hurry. Well, he paid Dad with fresh twenties when it was time. Then he was gone. The men in the shop was talking about him when a guy come down out of the office and says, You know who he was, don't you? And the men pretty much said, naw, they didn't have a clue. And the office guy says, He's that fellow from Sallisaw the papers call Pretty Boy Floyd. Well, you hear a lot of people say they seen Pretty Boy Floyd back in them days. Most of them are just feeding you a line. But you know what? I think it was him. I really do. . . .

11

We never studied stars.

The night lights that interested us pierced the sky from distant black
horizons. Drilling rigs. Most impressive were the big triples, tall enough
to handle three jointed lengths of drill stem. If we had a symbol of hope,
that was it. Hire on as a weevil/worm, and do all the shit work on the rig
floor. If you survived and proved your worth, you became a floor hand.
Then, if you really stuck with it, you might become the derrick hand, the
man up on top of the rig, guiding stands of pipe when the drill stem is
tripped, the man charged with monitoring the fluids from the mud pits
and other important tasks. And then the chance to become the driller,
the team leader. And then beyond that, tool pusher—the dream
position, the boss of all the crews (the towers) on all the rigs.

The old man understood those lights.

He knew about promise.

He knew about promise denied.

His work career and his memories kicked off simultaneously. Before he
began to struggle with learning letters and numbers, he was mounted on
the back of the lead mule of a team, tickling its nose with a feather tied
to the end of stick. From that beginning, he worked until his body
completely collapsed. When he was reduced to shuffling instead of
walking, when he was all but completely blind, he still kept at it, making
beds, folding laundry. I never saw work as something he loved. Just the
opposite. He was a gladiator in the pit. This battle never knew a fiercer
warrior. He worked and worked and worked because not to do so would
be surrender. To something. I'm not sure just what the something was.
Or wasn't.

For the most part, school was a bother; it stood in the way of working.
When he was a child, he labored away at farm chores. By the time he
was in junior high, he was an employee in the garage at the local Ford
dealership, learning the mechanic's trade under his father's tutelage. "I
had exactly twenty minutes," he told me once, "to make it from Fogarty

Junior High to the dealership and change my clothes and be working. That's a mile and two blocks. So, you know, I was hustling my butt the whole way." The dealership was open from early in the morning until evening Monday through Saturday and half a day on Sunday. He was expected to be there when it was open, except for those hours when he was in school. None of this relieved him of his farm chores. He was up before dawn every day to tend to those. There was no time for homework—besides, his undiagnosed lazy eye had already damaged his vision to the point that reading didn't come easily. School became an obstacle to real life. Real life was work.

The pace continued into high school. Work at the Ford garage, work on the farm. He somehow made time for FFA and showed a steer at the county fair and at spring livestock shows. He was good at it. His steer was a grand champion. With the backing of a local banker, he went on to show it at big shows in places like Kansas City. But he was never freed from his jobs. World War II had broken out, and he and his buddies figured they'd be Army-bound as soon as they graduated.

He also roughnecked some. With men off to war, there were plenty of jobs for high school boys in the oilfield. You could work morning tower (midnight to eight a.m.), drag yourself to class, nod off during school work, cut up after school let out, maybe drink a beer or two, sleep a little, then head back to the rig.

The war ended a year before he graduated.

When he turned eighteen, he went in for his military physical, only to be told he couldn't have served anyway because of his bad eyesight.

He had dreams.

They would be crushed almost as quickly as he could dream them.

12.

His father was his hero. I never knew him. A heart attack dropped him while he was still in his fifties, maybe a couple of years before the old man and Mom met and started dating. If the old man had a guiding light, it went black the day his father died. I've seen photos of him, but I've never really been able to assemble him in my mind. He was a thin man, bald, typically had a small cancer on his lip from his cigarette (the old man never smoked himself). This Grandpa was authoritarian and was considered all-wise, at least within the family. He farmed and mechanicked, either as shop foreman at the Ford garage or running his own garage.

There was a kind of split I never understood in the family. The old man and one of his brothers were aligned with his father; another brother and a sister allied themselves with their mother. I don't understand, but I do. His mother, whom I did know, unfortunately, was nightjar crazy and stung like a yellowjacket. And, Lord, was she judgmental, enough to put the brimstone spewing prophets of the Old Testament to shame. She refused to speak to her own brother for more than forty years because he committed the sin of marrying a Catholic. Another family chasm she created prohibited the old man from ever meeting his cousins, the only siblings in the Baseball Hall of Fame. And it was she who denied the old man's request to play high school football, in part on the grounds that athletes were not decent people. Praise the Lord and pass the Pepper Martin.

But his father—this character could make you straighten up and fly right in a hurry. He showed you what toughness meant. He was once crushed between a truck and a wall, spent months in a body cast, and came back to work again. That was what I heard for years and years. But then, in later years, the old man told me how his father struggled to control him, how he was helpless to do anything about it when the old man made a prick of himself a few times at the Ford garage. He told me about the time when, frustrated by the old man's drinking, his father climbed the stairs to Dee Freeman's apartment. "Just one thing I ask of you, Dee," he said. "Just try to make sure no one sells him anything if he's already drunk." Dee said he'd do what he could.

Later, when I was broke and felt washed up, living in a trailer house of my own and married to a woman I didn't love and driving a piece of shit pickup, I spent some time in the old man's shop, borrowing his tools to keep my pickup running awhile longer. (I never could mechanic worth a damn, always hated it.) One day, I finished up my work and was getting ready to leave when the old man walked over and leaned against the pickup's fender and started talking. The conversation took some odd turns. He kept directing us back to his childhood.

I never thought I was any good at showing you boys how to do stuff. No one ever showed me. It was the way Dad done me. You don't know what it was like. He expected you to learn things on your own, and if you didn't have it figured out, he made you feel like a piece of shit. I mean, he made you feel like you was worthless. You don't know what it was like.

This, about the man he loved and respected above all others. No, I never could know what that was like. Or why.

13.

Here are some things the old man never showed me how to do.

Throw a baseball. Throw a football. Throw a punch. Block a punch. Shoot a duck. Clean a fish. Shave. Bait a hook. Tie on a leader. Tie a square knot. Tie a tie. Dress the way a man should dress. Shine shoes. Sharpen a knife. Plane wood. Hang sheet rock. Fix plumbing. Patch bicycle tire. Open a checking account. Buy stock. Invest in real estate.

He did give me some useful tips on bowling, but I learned more from Easy Newman, who operated Uptown Lanes in my hometown.

And there was weirdness.

He tried to show me how to drive a pickup with a manual transmission, and all I could do was kill the engine every time I let off the clutch. Over and over and over. His disgust was a vapor that filled the truck's cab. Yet, I could go out to the country with friends, and drive standard transmission flatbed trucks and pickups in hayfields and along dirt roads, and never have an issue. I couldn't understand why.

He tried to show me how to waterski at Lake Tenkiller. I never could get up and stay up. Up, then down. Up, then down. Up, then down. (My stepbrothers, of course, were naturals at it.) And yet I went skiing with friends on the muddy waters of Lake Carl Blackwell and never had any trouble getting up and staying up, even jumping the wake.

I suppose I thought my role was to be the family failure. And I was adept at living up to it. What I was good at were things unvalued in our home. School, for one thing. I was kind of a juvenile delinquent, yet I always made good grades and liked learning. I may have skipped class in the eighth grade to smoke weed on the roof of the junior high shop building, but I found American history to be interesting as all get out—and English literature even more so.

None of the grades I brought home impressed the old man. I acted in plays and performed in concerts, but he never attended a single one. He did not show up for my high school graduation. I finished as president of the student body, with the third highest GPA in my class. He spent that night in his shop, with his wrenches and air-compressor and jacks.

14.

Oh, I thought I had it worked out. I was driving for Halliburton and mechanicking for them, too. But they figured out I couldn't see out of one eye. That pretty well ended things. I was going to make some real money, but, no, they told me I couldn't even back a truck out of the shop with my vision like it was. Insurance. Goddamn insurance. It's the ruin of about everything. This one fellow, he talked to me about a Halliburton job there in Duncan, inside a building. It was nothing but offices, and you was inside all day. I couldn't see myself an office man. No, no way. So me and Halliburton come to a parting of the ways.

I went to work for the aircraft manufacturer in Fort Worth, and that was going to be a sweet deal. You was on contract for ninety days, and then they decided if they wanted to keep you on permanent. Well, everything about that company and that job was great. Good retirement plan, everything. I worked my old butt off. I wanted that job. After sixty days, they had those of us who had more or less made the grade come in for a physical. I didn't know, but a requirement for the permanent job was 20/20 vision. They tested my eyes along with everything else, and I figured I was okay because no one said nothing to me. I went on back to work the next day, and it was just like always. About ten days later, the old foreman saw me and said, What in the hell are you doing here? I told him I was just working. He said, Well, didn't they tell you you couldn't have a permanent job because of your eyesight? And I said, Naw, no one said a word. He told me I was free to work out the rest of the ninety day contract, but I should probably head on and find a job somewhere else because they wouldn't have permanent work for me. So I headed on back to Oklahoma. My mind wasn't in too good a place after that. . . .

15

And it went to a worse place.

Punk Ferris, my high school counselor, grew up with the old man and his first wife, Ramona. He told me they were as unalike as bologna and angel food, even aside from their age difference. What brought them together beat him. Beats me as well. Ramona, of course, was just a kid. Before she turned twenty, she gave birth to two children in eighteen months. But she was wild and impetuous, qualities that I saw still resided in her when she was in middle age. I heard stories about her and her failures as a teenage mom. I don't know if they are true.

But I know the old man wound up with sole custody of his two sons—something that almost never happened in the 1950s, a man winning custody. I know that the old man felt nothing but bitterness for fifty years after they split up.

So, there he was.

He couldn't get a job he wanted.

He couldn't free himself from the small town he ached to leave.

He went through the bitterest of divorces and wound up with two pre-school sons to raise.

His hope was for his father to guide him through his troubles. Then his dad up and died in McAlester, Oklahoma, just days after getting a clean bill of health from the family doctor.

The old man took over his dad's auto repair business. His whacked out mother helped him with the boys. He seethed and looked at the world as a place that had fucked him over royally. "There was about two years after Dad died," he told me once, "that I just can't remember. Everything is a blank about them to me." But those two years molded the next six decades of his life.

16.

On a winter's day, one devoid of any color, he sits in a dim living room, talking to me as the wind howls around the house.

"If you work on cars for a living," he says, "people look at you like you are the lowest of the low. At least, that's how it is in this town. I imagine that's how it is everywhere."

In that instant, I thought about how he must have felt about his mechanic father and mechanic grandfather. And I thought about how he must have felt about his mechanic self every morning when he slipped on his greasy coveralls and tromped out the door.

17.

He is in a skilled nursing center for now but will be moved soon to a nursing home. Mom is attempting to maintain a twenty-hour-a-day vigil with him. He is less violent, more cooperative with the staff when she is there. But he's shitting on himself and talking about cars from the 1960s.

The 1960s—one gift I received from him was music. In my office hang three of the first four LPs Johnny Cash released, the very records he'd play in our trailer house. And there were albums by Carl Smith, Elvis, and Carl Perkins. Hank Williams was a kind of god, his music treated as holy. Bob Wills was spoken of in hushed, respectful tones. We always had a lot of black music in our house, too, and I'm not sure many white people from that time and place can make that claim. Mom's love was country, but the old man dug what was then called "race music." So there were long-players by Bo Diddley, Lloyd Price, Ray Charles, Fats Domino, and Little Richard.

In my hometown, at the Melba Theatre, white folks sat downstairs; black folks, up in the buzzard's roost balcony. The Townhouse Restaurant had a sign in the front window that read "We reserve the right to refuse service to anyone," which meant no black people could dine there. Signs at the courthouse and county fairgrounds still designated "white" and "colored" restrooms. Harrison Avenue ran east and west from city limit to city limit. No name was given to the part of town north of Harrison, but south of Harrison was prosaically known as "niggertown." I attended segregated schools from the first through the sixth grade.

The old man never was much of one for honkytonking. Instead, he preferred what he called "nigger-jointing." He and his buddies frequented the bars and restaurants south of Harrison. In particular, Rick's Place, where he'd drink Red Cap ale, flirt innocently with the black waitresses, and plug nickels into the jukebox to hear B.B. King or Bobby "Blue" Bland.

By the time Mom and I came along, his favorite dining spot was Harriett's. What a marvel that place was. It's official name was the H&A

Supper Club, but no one ever called it that. Just Harriett's, after the proprietor, a black woman named Harriett Kennedy. Harriett's sat across the street from the black high school, and it was home to steaks that came out sizzling on metal plates, impeccable barbecue ribs, and the best fried shrimp and chicken I've ever eaten. Harriett served beer, and she provided set-ups if you wanted to bring in a bottle, which the old man typically did.

"Freddy!" Harriett would call as soon as she saw the old man enter the door. That was not his name, but she got to call him Freddy. "Freddy, you come on in here right now!" At the sound of her voice, the old man would light up and grin like a four-year-old at an Easter egg hunt. She'd direct us to a table or booth, and as soon as a waitress had taken our order, Harriett would come sit with us, scooting in next to the old man and giving him a hug. "Freddy, sugar, how are you doing? And how's this pretty wife of yours? And these boys?" The old man's face would get brighter and brighter with each word she spoke. In the background, Ray Charles would be singing about Jack hitting the road, and all around us white people and black people would be dining shoulder-to-shoulder, and everyone thought it was just fine. Harriett's was the center of sanity in that town.

I'm thinking now about how much genuine affection Harriett and the old man had for each other. I'm thinking about how many black customers the old man had when he ran his auto repair business. I'm thinking about the time the retired principal of the black high school was talking to me—this, after I was a grown man—and realized whose boy I was: "Let me tell you something about him. A colored man could take his vehicle in to him to be fixed, and he would treat him fair, do his best work, charge the same thing he'd charge a white man. I can't say that about many white businessmen in this town. But your dad? Yes."

But then there's the Black Cats episode. Every June, our family put up a fireworks stand on Oklahoma Avenue to earn a little money for school clothes. When I was maybe in the fourth grade, I was left alone in charge of the stand. That day, a group of kids, all much older and from south of Harrison Avenue, came to the stand. I'm guessing there may have been ten in all. They all began talking at once. Some began reaching for fireworks from the sides of the stand. Some crawled over the makeshift front counter and grabbed at the goods on display. I darted back and forth, trying to keep up with what was going on.

All of a sudden, the old man came hustling down from his shop. When he did, the kids took off running. I could see packages of Black Cat firecrackers stuck in their pockets and waistlines as they ran.

The old man entered the stand and unloaded on me. How could I stand there and let them steal from me? Was I just going to let people take stuff from me all my life? What the hell was wrong with me?

In my mind, there wasn't much I could do. I was outnumbered, and they were all older, junior high and high school boys.

He started to stomp away but turned around. "And they were niggers! How could you let niggers steal from you? Goddamn niggers! Niggers! What in the hell is wrong with you?"

I've hated fireworks since that day.

18

And so it went.

Sometimes okay, sometimes not. Mostly not.

One sweltering summer day, Mom left me at the house with our next door neighbor, Vic—I'm not sure where my stepbrothers were. She told me to close up the house and turn on the window-mounted air-conditioner around 2 p.m., which I did. Maybe fifteen minutes after the AC began grinding away, the front door flew open. The old man stood trembling with some kind of mysterious rage before Vic and me, sweat and blood from a new cut streaming down his face, spittle dripping from the corner of his mouth.

"Don't you think," he all but roared, "I don't know what's going on. Because I do, buddy. Goddamn, I do. Mister, I'll put your ass out on the street!"

"What did I do?"

He shouted at me to shut up. "You know what you did. You keep this old shit up, and you'll hurt in ways you can't imagine!"

Then he slammed the door behind him. A picture slid from the living room wall. Vic and I looked at each other wordlessly. To this day, I have no idea why he was pissed off. Vic took off pretty quickly. He didn't come over to the house much after that.

When Mom returned home, I told her what happened. She stared at me and spoke not a word. Later, she left again. Alone in the house, I did the only thing that made sense at the time: I put Hank Williams on the stereo, understanding all too well the impulse to jump in the river and drown.

The old man startled me when he came in the front door. Now, he was quiet. Or at least as quiet as he ever was. As soon as he entered, I hustled over to the stereo and turned off the music.

"No, no," he said. "Leave it on."

I dropped the needle back on the black vinyl. Is this when he beats the crap out of me? Maybe knocks out a couple of teeth? Maybe fractures a bone? He walked into the kitchen like a little boy seeking a lost puppy. I heard him drop ice cubes into one of those jelly glasses and fill it—this time with tap water. He ambled into the living room once more and leaned against the wall, his eyes closed, and nodded along as Hank sang about sleeping in the doghouse. I waited for him to say something, but he just nodded. Then he took his ice water and retreated to the shop.

Nothing was ever said about the incident.

By anyone.

19.

That shop of Dad's next to Mother's house—it wasn't big enough. And we had the trailer on her place—and it wasn't big enough. None of it was going to work out. So I gave it a lot of thought, just how I could make things work. Then five acres come up for sale a couple of blocks down the street. I knew that property would work. It had a house on it, and there was room to put up a shop building. It was just a matter of if I could pull it together. So I went to see the people at both banks. They weren't interested in giving me the time of day. Just wouldn't even listen to me. So I didn't know what I was going to do. Finally, I went down and saw the owner of the Ford dealership. I sat right across from him and explained what I wanted to do with this garage business, and he listened to it all and said, That plan of yours will work. But then he said he didn't mess around with investing in something as small as what I had in mind. Now, by this point, he had offshore drilling rigs and was drilling in Canada, too. Plus, he had stuff going on in Louisiana. So you might say I was just too small a fish. I guess he saw how disappointed I was, and he said, You give me a little time. You call the First State Bank at 2 o'clock this afternoon. You talk to them then. Well, I did, and everything was different. We pretty well had things closed that day. We never would have had this place if it hadn't been for that old man. . . .

20.

I dropped deeply within myself as months, then years crawled past. My older stepbrother fought more wars and was accorded more battle medals. But then something happened. When he was around fifteen, he left home, moved to Fort Worth to live with his mother. I heard it was maybe because he wanted to live in Texas because there you could get a driver's license much earlier than you could in Oklahoma. I heard it was because his mother would allow him to smoke in the house. But I was never sure exactly why. It was okay with me. I didn't mind having him gone from the house. And when we went to visit him, I was able to go to Six Flags Over Texas and ride the log flume.

And my younger stepbrother.

At some point, something coded within him kicked in, and he began to change.

Twenty-five years later, after I'd moved to Texas myself, I held his hand as he lay semi-conscious in an Arlington, Texas, ICU. A ventilator breathed for him, his lungs ruined by pneumocystis pneumonia. Ugly lesions covered his chest. I knew, his mother knew, his half-sister knew, his partner knew, the doctors and staff at the hospital knew, but no one else. He told the medical providers not to say anything to anyone. "He is just so afraid that his dad will find out he's gay," his partner told me. I thought, How could the old man not know? But the family had nested itself in so many layers of secrets and denials over the years that maybe he had refused to recognize what had been so plainly obvious for so many years.

I knew in that instant that I had to make the call to Oklahoma, that I had to tell my parents their son was dying of AIDS. (Had my parents not wondered why they hadn't seen him in two years?) I would have to tell them he hadn't contracted it through a transfusion or anything like that, but through unprotected gay sex. I left his partner and ICU to make the phone call.

A month later, after the funeral, I was ready to head back to Texas. The old man stopped me and said, "You know, this has shown me we have a pretty damned good family. You done right down there in Fort Worth. You called us and got your momma and me down there before he died. You took a hold of things. I'll always appreciate it."

With one of his huge, horn-hard hands, he patted me on the back.

Things were always workable between us after that.

21

The move to the nursing home will occur in three days. The doctor has told Mom he will never get better. He will never be able to return home.

"It's so hard to see him like this," she says.

I understand.

I know he's in agony. He wants to die on that five acres he bought decades ago. All those years: out of bed and a quick breakfast, then unlock the shop at 7 or 7:30. Come down to the house for a sandwich at noon. Break for supper at 6. Go back to the shop and finish up jobs until 8 or 9, sometimes 10. Put in at least half a day on Saturday. Spend most of Sunday cleaning up the shop. Or brush-hogging grass. Or rototilling the garden patch. More and more. He lived his fullest life on this patch of earth; he should die here. But he can't. Instead, his final breath will come in a strange bed amid the stench of piss and disinfectant. I wish I could give him the gift of death where he wants it,.

It's hard-ass country up there. Tornados, wildfires, earthquakes, blizzards, scorching droughts. Dust is everywhere. Skunks are everywhere. Ticks thrive in lawns and gardens. The people are tough, sometimes underhanded and violent. The old man survived it all, clawed out a life. He clawed me, too. He clawed everyone who came too close.

I think about him constantly these days.

I think about the time he told me over the phone how much he appreciated the Merle Haggard albums I'd given him in recent years. He'd never paid much attention to Haggard until I started sending the CDs his way. I think about how much he hated Kris Kristofferson the first time he heard him but how, over the years, Kristofferson became one of his favorites—he sings like a regular guy.

I think about the time I won an Oklahoma Book Award. The day after the ceremony, the old man sat at his dining room table and fingered the medal I'd been given the evening before. He took out his thickest magnifying glass and positioned himself so he could read the inscription on the back. Say, fella—this is quite something. You can go back in this family as far as you can, and nobody's ever won something like this. You've done something here.

I think about that last time we talked at length, sitting at the same dining room table. He revisited the old stories one more time: Dee Freeman the bootlegger, the roughnecking expedition to Snyder. Like most storytellers or jam band musicians, he improvised. In this telling, the fight in Snyder did not involve knives but machetes.

I think about that night, and I think about what I've inherited from him. I pay bills on time and am fanatic about filing taxes when they're due. I stick money back, and I eschew consumer debt—things I learned from him. I try to be square in my business dealings, another lesson from him. I work hard, though not nearly as hard as the master. But I'm not right in the head. I never have been. I battle insecurity, paranoia, depression, and fear, and I know he's responsible for instilling much of this in me. I'm cynical and at times judgmental and often come across harsh as horseradish—traits I picked up from him.

And anger—well, you get the picture.

Tonight, I find myself breaking the seal on a fifth of Old Forester Kentucky Straight Bourbon Whiskey I bought at the liquor store up the street. The label is nothing like what I remember from my youth, but it's the real deal. I don't have any Coca-Cola for a mixer, and I haven't used a jelly jar for a glass in forever. I'll drink from an iced tea tumbler. I fill it half full, no ice, and gulp down most of it in a way I think would impress anyone who wrestles pig iron for a living. My throat and belly burn.

He's dying up there in red dirt country, and here I am, trying to prove something.

CPSIA information can be obtained
at www.ICGtesting.com
Printed in the USA
FSHW011050280119
55309FS

9 781942 956075